D1272920

AMAZING SNAKES!

INLAND TAIPANS

BY CHRIS BOWMAN

EPIC

BELLWETHER MEDIA • MINNEAPOLIS, MN

EPIC BOOKS are no ordinary books. They burst with intense action, high-speed heroics, and shadows of the unknown. Are you ready for an Epic adventure?

This edition first published in 2014 by Bellwether Media, Inc.

No part of this publication may be reproduced in whole or in part without written permission of the publisher. For information regarding permission, write to Bellwether Media, Inc., Attention: Permissions Department, 5357 Penn Avenue South, Minneapolis, MN 55419.

Library of Congress Cataloging-in-Publication Data

Bowman, Chris, 1990- author.
  Inland Taipans / by Chris Bowman.
      pages cm. – (Epic. Amazing Snakes!)
  Summary: "Engaging images accompany information about inland taipans. The combination of high-interest subject matter and light text is intended for students in grades 2 through 7"– Provided by publisher.
  Audience: Ages 7-12.
  Audience: Grades 2 to 7.
  Includes bibliographical references and index.
  ISBN 978-1-62617-124-4 (hardcover : alk. paper)
  1. Oxyuranus–Juvenile literature. 2. Elapidae–Juvenile literature. I. Title.
  QL666.O64B69 2014
  597.96'4–dc23
                                                                  2013050261

TABLE OF CONTENTS

WHAT ARE INLAND TAIPANS?

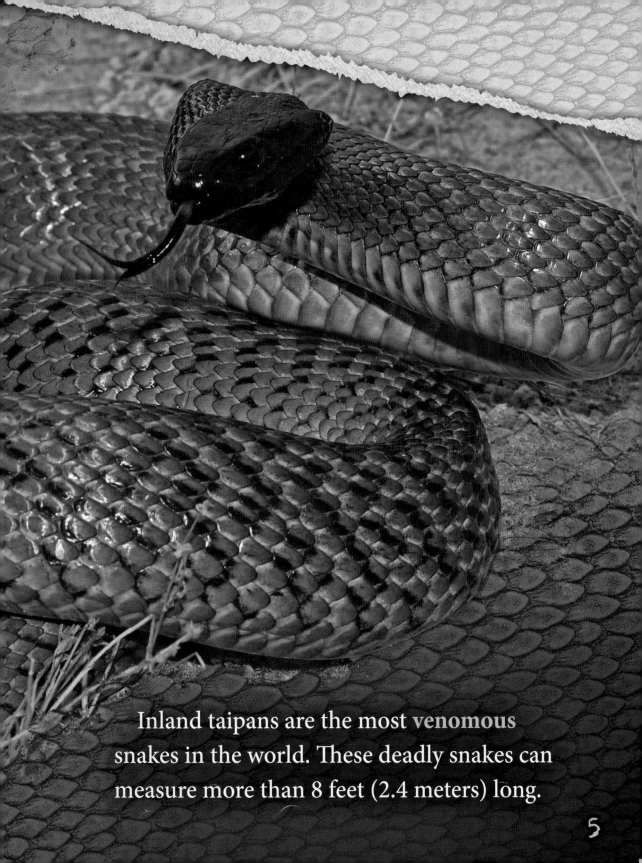

Inland taipans are the most venomous snakes in the world. These deadly snakes can measure more than 8 feet (2.4 meters) long.

WHERE INLAND TAIPANS LIVE

inland taipan range = ▭

Inland taipans live in the Australian outback.
It is very hot there. The snakes must escape the heat.
They hide in burrows and cracks in the ground.

HANDLING HEAT

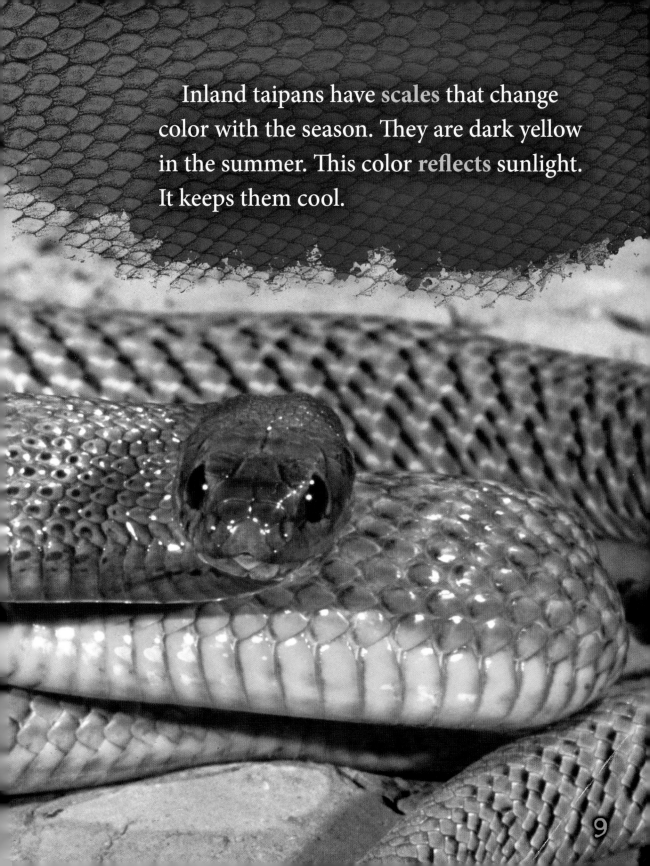

Inland taipans have **scales** that change color with the season. They are dark yellow in the summer. This color **reflects** sunlight. It keeps them cool.

Their scales turn brown and black in the winter. These colors soak in sunlight. This keeps inland taipans warm. Scale colors also **camouflage** the snakes in the outback.

PREDATORS AND PREY

king brown snake

Inland taipans are shy snakes with few enemies. They like to avoid attackers rather than fight them. Their only known **predator** is the king brown snake.

All Bark, No Bite?

Inland taipans are deadly snakes. However, no human has ever died from an inland taipan bite.

14

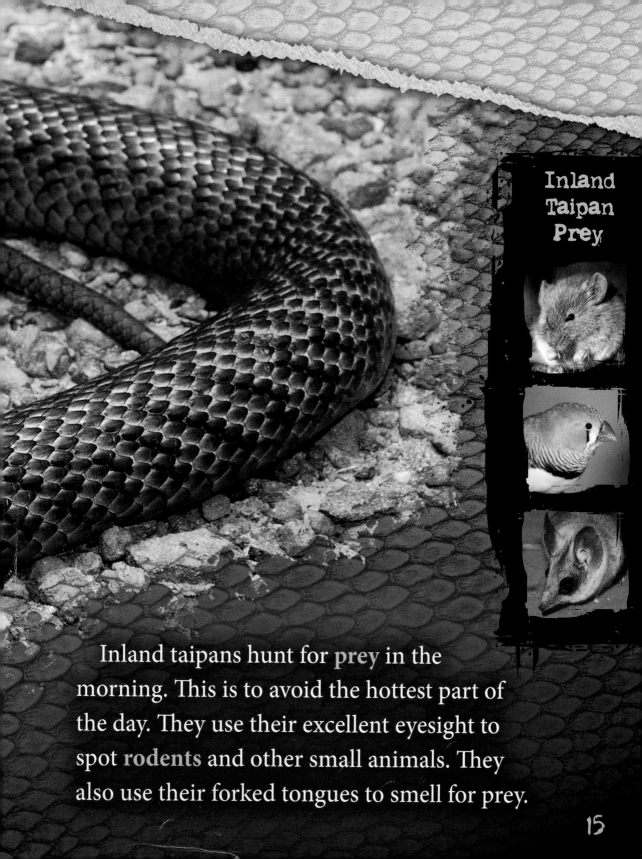

Inland
Taipan
Prey

Inland taipans hunt for **prey** in the morning. This is to avoid the hottest part of the day. They use their excellent eyesight to spot **rodents** and other small animals. They also use their forked tongues to smell for prey.

15

The inland taipan traps an animal in a burrow. It attacks its meal with its **fangs**. Its strong **venom** kills the animal before it can fight back.

Packs a Punch

One inland taipan bite is powerful enough to kill 100 people.

The snake stretches its jaws wide.
Then it swallows the animal whole.
Its venom even helps it **digest** its meal!

SPECIES PROFILE

SCIENTIFIC NAME:	*OXYURANUS MICROLEPIDOTUS*
NICKNAMES:	WESTERN TAIPAN, SMALL-SCALED SNAKE, FIERCE SNAKE
AVERAGE SIZE:	5.9-8.2 FEET (1.8-2.5 METERS)
HABITAT:	OUTBACK
RANGE:	AUSTRALIA
VENOMOUS:	YES
HUNTING METHOD:	VENOMOUS BITE
COMMON PREY:	RATS, MICE, KULTARRS, MOLES, SHREWS, BIRDS

GLOSSARY

burrows—homes dug in the ground by animals

camouflage—to hide an animal by helping it blend in with the surroundings

digest—to break food down

fangs—sharp, hollow teeth; venom flows through fangs and into a bite.

outback—the wilderness regions of Australia located in the middle of country

predator—an animal that hunts other animals for food

prey—animals that are hunted by other animals for food

reflects—shines light back

rodents—small animals that usually gnaw on their food

scales—small plates of skin that cover and protect a snake's body

venom—a poison created by a snake; snakes use venom to hurt or kill other animals.

venomous—able to create venom in their bodies; inland taipans release venom through their fangs.

TO LEARN MORE

At the Library

Bishop, Nic. *Snakes*. New York, N.Y.: Scholastic Nonfiction, 2012.

Stewart, Melissa. *Snakes!* Washington, D.C.: National Geographic, 2009.

Sweazey, Davy. *Death Adders*. Minneapolis, Minn.: Bellwether Media, 2014.

On the Web

Learning more about inland taipans is as easy as 1, 2, 3.

1. Go to www.factsurfer.com.

2. Enter "inland taipans" into the search box.

3. Click the "Surf" button and you will see a list of related web sites.

With factsurfer.com, finding more information is just a click away.

INDEX